TRAFFIC SIGNS

on the

ROAD OF LIFE

WILBUR & CYNTHIA BROWER

Library of Congress Card Catalog Number: 2012919647

Brower, Wilbur L.
Brower, Cynthia W.

Traffic Signs on the Road of Life

1. Self-help 2. Inspirational 3. Motivational
4. Personal Development 5. Spiritual

Correspondence to the authors should be directed to:

P. O. Box 195
Comfort, NC 28522
Phone: (910) 548-0698
E-mail: wlbrower@gmail.com

ISBN: 978-0-9884490-0-8

Dedication

We dedicate this effort to all on the Road of Life who have not yet paid heed to the traffic signs that will assist them in having a prosperous, productive and safe journey. It is our sincere hope that this little book will help them to discern the signs and the times and to fulfill the promise and power of their life's journey.

Contents

Foreword

Every once in a while, you read a book that completely changes how you think about your life, igniting within you a new impetus to be more, do more and give more. This is that kind of book. An inspiring guide to the one thing we all want: more life in our lives. It is a perceptive, thoughtful and richly illustrated look in the dramatic personification of symbols of all sorts. *Traffic Signs on the Road of Life* is an eye-opening insight into the troubling times that many in this nation are experiencing as a result of not adhering to these and other signs. The Browers launched an insightful and well-written masterpiece that provokes the reader to look at the everyday, everywhere symbols that govern and control the cosmos and cause us to see beyond the literal words and symbols. This book is for everyone, because every person, at some point in life, has desperately wished for sound, experienced guidance while trying to navigate the treacherous waters of a personal, professional or business crisis, be it large or small. With Traffic Signs, Cynthia and Wil provide clear and concise admonitions for successfully maneuvering through life and how to handle dire situations. They have richly illuminated important truths that are seen daily and have given them personal application. A superb and integral read that evokes all readers with a myriad of experiences to take heed to the 'traffic signs on the road of life' in order to better enjoy life's excursions.

Dr. Thomas L. Stewart

Preface

It is rare that a book comes along that gives the reader a jolt from every phrase or thought read or heard, and causes her or him to stare with wonder, in a profoundly personal way, at the simplicity and relevance of that information; but *Traffic Signs on the Road of Life*_does exactly that. In the same vein as *A Little Book of Big Principles—Values and Virtues for a More Successful Life* (1998), Dr. Wil Brower, again, has produced a self-help and personal development masterpiece worthy of mention in the same sentence as works from gurus such as Robert Allen, Napoleon Hill, Jim Rohn, and Brain Tracey, and Napoleon Hill, all masters of blueprints and templates for achieving personal and professional success.

In addition to being a guide for establishing, building and maintaining our momentum on our life's journey, *Traffic Signs on the Road of Life* is also a book that will challenge you and change the way you view the world and your place and purpose in it. Each lesson, which is built around traffic signs that are commonplace in our daily living, will not allow you to see traffic signs the same again. Some will remind you of lessons you learned during your travel but didn't know at the time what they meant. Others will speak into your life "learnings" that will prepare you for many challenges and opportunities that have not yet come your way. Either way, the lessons comprise a power-packed little book that is sure to amaze and transform you at the same time.

Traffic Signs on the Road of Life is guaranteed to cause you to marvel at its simplicity and make you hang on to and cherish every word of its wisdom. You can't resist reading it numerous times because of the lessons that are hidden during the first reading and will not be revealed until you've looked at traffic signs with a new eye and deeper understanding and thought about them for a few days, a few weeks or a few months. It is then that you will appreciate the lessons and their relevance in your life.

However, it is a book whose lessons are worthy of sharing with others, and a book you may even want to pass on to those you know will benefit from it, no matter at which milepost they are along life's journey. You and they will be better travelers for including the lessons in your traveling plans, because they will make the remainder of the journey infinitely more pleasurable and predictable.

Acknowledgements

It is rare that the mere mention of a project of this nature could resonate so powerfully with some many individuals from so many different backgrounds and walks of life. But, it did. Most of our friends and colleagues who heard of it were quick to ask if they could have first dibs on reading it and giving us feedback. We were just as quick to accept their offers. They have been most generous with their time and comments, and have provided us insights, reactions and thoughts that focused our thinking and gave us new ways of looking at and writing about many of the signs. For this, we are most grateful, because, without their input, the final product would not have achieved the level of perfection that it has.

We owe special thanks to Ms. Pat Jones and Mr. Esau Waters (LTC. US Air Force Retired) for providing us insightful feedback; and we owe Ms. Janet Thomas a special debt of gratitude for her significant contributions to the final iteration of this project. All of you went well beyond all of our expectations with the attention and care you gave this project. Your encouragement and insights made our work infinitely more enjoyable and rewarding, and they allowed us to rest peacefully with the assurance that our approach to this effort was not totally off the mark.

Any shortcomings related to this project are ours alone, and we will accept them as learning experiences that will make us more committed to and stronger in our work for the kingdom. If only one person on the Road of Life learns something from anything stated, or gains an insight from any analogy, comment or metaphor offered, we feel that our work will have been worth all the effort.

Have you not asked those who travel the road?

And do you not know their signs?

Job 21:29

Introduction: Know the Signs

Traffic signs, ever-present but often ignored, are devices placed along, beside, or above highways, freeways, roadways, pathways, or any other routes to guide, warn, regulate and inform the flow of traffic, including motor vehicles, pedestrians and other travelers.

Traffic signs tell us about traffic rules, hazards, where we are, how to get where we are going, and pleasures and pains we are likely to encounter along the way...

While many of the signs are words, many are only symbols that are universally recognized and understood by the attentive observer. Whether signs are words or symbols, they serve five basic functions:

- Fulfill a need
- Command attention
- Convey a clear, simple meaning
- Command respect from travelers
- Give adequate time for proper response

Therefore, the primary purpose of traffic signs is to warn, direct or regulate the flow of traffic and to inform. The shapes and colors of signs are important to ensure that they will capture the attention of the traveler. The signs must also be simple in order to be understood by all travelers, including foreign travelers who may be unfamiliar with the spoken language of the region in which they are traveling.

Traffic signs must be posted so that sufficient time is allotted for an adequate response by the traveler to do anything that the traveler is expected to do. Thus, signs must be positioned according to the results of engineering studies dictated by the facts. If signs are not warranted or are ineffective, they could divert the attention of the drivers from the more important traffic control devices. This could cause a disregard for all signs and could result in a waste of public agency and taxpayers' resources. Signs must be positioned so that they are essential for the safety and correct regulation of traffic in the area. If there are too many signs in any one area, people may take them for granted, and signs in that area could prove to be ineffective.

Traffic signs, signals and markings are provided and utilized to convey messages to road users. These devices are used for the purpose of establishing a user-friendly street and road system that is adequately and clearly understood by all users thereof. Road traffic signs may either contain **regulations** or **instructions** we are required to obey; **warnings** of hazards that may not be apparent; **markings** and **information guides** are about routes, destinations and points of interest or leisure activities we might want to consider. There are many parallels between traffic signs posted on the roadways and the traffic signs that, figuratively speaking, are posted on the Road of

Life. Like the signs on the roads that we often ignore, we also often choose to ignore the signs on the Road of Life. Many times on the Road of Life, we often find ourselves similar to a foreign traveler, going over terrains that are unfamiliar to us and signs that are difficult to decipher. We find ourselves in situations we've never before encountered or experienced and, therefore, are sure how to respond to them. We are not foreigners because we don't know or understand the signs. Rather, we are foreigners because we've chosen to ignore them.

Pilot Car — Follow Me

An Escort, Flag or Pilot Car is a vehicle that serves as an extension of the traffic warning system and accompanies it through a specific area. Typically, Escort, Flag and Pilot cars are for wide loads, oversized loads, for truckers and all loads requiring permits because of their size, weight and width.

PILOT CAR
FOLLOW ME

Pilot Cars are usually operating in areas where roads are being constructed or are being repaired. It is the Pilot Car's duty to guide us safely through the construction or repair areas and, in effect, deposit us securely where and when it is safe for us to travel alone. There is no mistaking Pilot Cars. They are clearly marked and often even have the additional command, Follow Me, displayed prominently. If we fail to follow the Pilot Car, we are left to get through difficult and untenable situations the best way that we can. If we get stuck, hit rough spots or run off the road because we did not follow the Pilot Car, it is our own fault.

These pilot cars must have flags, signs, and lights on the car to warn the public that there is an oversized load coming through. These cars clear the way or run interference for the load that follows. In essence, they are the eyes and ears leading the way. Traveling is infinitely more challenging, but not impossible, when a Pilot Car is desperately needed but one is not available.

In addition to being the Pilot Car for us to follow, God also has erected all the necessary Traffic Signs on the Road of Life to facilitate and guide our journey. It is up to us to feel, hear and see those instructions, warnings, markings and information guides prominently displayed for us to obey and follow. Even when the traffic signs are invisible or less accessible than we would like them to be or they are only foreshadowed in the deeper recesses of our hearts and minds, God gave us the power to discern what lies ahead on our journey if we would only listen to the small whispers and yield to the gently tugs that fill us with His presence; they assure us of the appropriate courses of action we should take.

It is likely that we will struggle under the weight of many heavy, oversized and wide loads on the Road of Life, including disappointments, financial challenges and different kinds of personal losses. However, God's grace and mercy is always with us, no matter what circumstances present themselves to us or trials and tribulations that come along the way; and it is His grace and mercy that will sustain us. He has given us the authority, capacity and endurance to conquer them all. It is up to us to follow Him.

Regulatory / Instructions

Regulatory signs give us instructions, which impart authoritative directions, knowledge, or information; they remind us to check, monitor and control our natural behavior, base impulses and genuine human tendencies. They define the laws we must obey, and we must obey them unless we are willing to pay a heavy price. Such signs might even appear to be demanding, intrusive and dictatorial. However, they claim to know what is best for us when we may not know it ourselves. They remind us to acknowledge that we are not in control of our ultimate fate, no matter how hard we try. Our own arrogance and self-assuredness often blind us to those signs. Whether they are words or symbols, the signs are usually displayed or are flashing brightly before our eyes. We are inclined to ignore the signs of instructions that are meant especially for us, in a mistaken belief and sincere hope that we will not be caught violating any of the instructions or regulations.

Posted all along the Road of Life are many warning signs attempting to regulate our attitudes, thoughts and behaviors. These signs are not always as obvious to some of us as they are to others, but we know that if we violate them, we probably will be penalized. Some of us have not developed the sensibility or sensitivity to recognize that these signs can make our life markedly easier, and others acknowledge the signs but refuse to obey them. We often believe that the price we'd pay for disobeying the signs is less than the price we'd pay for changing our attitudes, thoughts and behaviors. This rationale is often embedded in mental scripts we've created from our earliest life experiences, which have a profound influence on what we hear, think and believe about ourselves and others.

If we stick to those mental scripts and refuse to consider other factors that might inform us and expand our view of the world, we never discover that what we always thought, heard and believed, about ourselves as well as others, might be all wrong.

Yield

A YIELD, or GIVE WAY, traffic sign indicates that each driver must prepare to stop if necessary to let a driver on another approach proceed. Yield signs are used in place of stop signs in instances where a complete stop may not be required. A driver who stops has yielded the right of way to another. In contrast, a stop sign requires each driver to stop completely before proceeding, even if no other traffic is present. Whenever a YIELD sign is present, it is our responsibility to slow down, look to the right or left and yield to oncoming traffic. Yield signs are the only shape traffic sign that is an equilateral triangle, meaning that all three sides are the same length. Yield signs are measured differently than other traffic signs, as they are unique in shape. They are measured by the length of the sides before the corners are rounded.

The YIELD is one of the most frequently misused traffic control devices, along with the STOP sign. Primary factors to be considered when judging the appropriateness of a YIELD sign to be used include traffic volumes, volume split, speeds, visibility, and crash history. The purpose of a yield sign is to assign right-of-way to traffic entering an intersection. Vehicles controlled by a yield sign need to slow down or stop when necessary to avoid interfering with conflicting traffic. The yield sign is also found at un-signaled railroad crossings where we must yield to approaching trains. Yield signs are used to protect traffic on one of two intersecting streets without requiring traffic on the other street to come to a complete stop. Studies indicate Yield signs are effective in certain low volume conditions with adequate sight distances. Some efficiencies in accident reduction, delays, and operating costs can be realized with the use of Yield signs. Yield signs have an advantage over stop signs in that they do not require traffic to stop. This results in much less delay, emissions, frustration, and non-compliance. Yield signs are installed at locations in which the ordinary rules of the road are not able to orderly facilitate traffic. We should not forcibly merge our vehicle into traffic if a yield sign is present and other vehicles have the right-of-way.

Yielding or giving way to others on the Road of Life is not always easy. In fact, it can be quite disconcerting and distressing if we live with the delusion that our individual progress and personal successes are the most important things in life. When we act and believe we are the center of the universe and that everything of any significance revolves around us, it's easy for us to become arrogant and selfish. Yielding to others is not in our realm of thinking. It's difficult for us to see that yielding can be a virtue; we often mistake and misperceive it as a vice or weakness. No matter how fast we need to get somewhere, caution should always be our watchword - and that is what a yield sign means to tell us.

Sometimes, we just need to slow down or wait, be quiet and consider others more than we consider ourselves.

Speed Limit

Road SPEED LIMIT signs are used in most countries to regulate the speed of road vehicles. Speed limits may define maximum (which may be variable), minimum or no speed limit. Speed limits are commonly set by the legislative bodies of nations or provincial governments and enforced by national or regional police and/or judicial bodies.

It is significant to note that the speed limit takes effect when we cross the imaginary line of the sign, not when we can actually see the sign.

It is often said that, in life, timing is everything. So, knowing when to increase or decrease the speed at which we do something is critical to the success of that effort. Also, it is important to know at what speed something should be done. It is often easy for us to become very excited about something and make a very hasty decision about it without weighing the pros and cons. In other instances, we can move too slowly on an opportunity when the speed limit demanded that we move at a quicker pace. Therefore, getting the speed and timing just right is critical to the success of business opportunities and effective and mutually beneficial interpersonal relationships. We have to look for the clues that will tell us the right speed for the circumstance or situation at hand. Because we are human, subject to the power of our emotions and self-interest, we are prone to act rashly and irrationally on a wide range of matters affecting us personally or in which we have vested interests.

In some areas, there are Minimum Speed signs, signaling that we can be penalized for moving too slowly for the road we're traveling. These signs are often accompanied by SLOWER TRAFFIC KEEP RIGHT signs. If we travel too slowly in a left lane, we pose grave dangers to ourselves and to other travelers. We travel under the illusion that our traveling cautiously in a left lane makes us a safer driver when, in fact, it makes us a more dangerous driver because we are impeding the flow of traffic and causing other travelers to determine how best to get passed us.

We often get in the easy flow of things because we are too cautious and methodical and, therefore, indecisive. We say we are trying to understand all the facts, but we become paralyzed by all the facts once we get and analyze them.

Do Not Enter

The sign DO NOT ENTER forewarns us of danger somewhere beyond the point at which the command was issued. Although the sign does not always tell what the danger is or might be, the command unmistakably is warning us to stay out for a reason. Sometimes, we can see or anticipate what is beyond the sign. Other times, we are clueless about the danger that lurks ahead. It we choose to venture into the area we've been asked not to enter, we do it at our own peril.

The DO NOT ENTER signs on the Road of Life are not always as clearly marked as are the typical signs. Nevertheless, we intuitively and instinctively know what most of the signs are. In those rare instances when we are uncertain about those DO NOT ENTER signs, we usually have enough commonsense, personal experience or knowledge of others' experience to know how far to venture into areas we sense are not good for us. We can get ourselves entangled and entrapped with many dangerous, debilitating and destructive situations for many years by "sampling" sins that get us addicted the first time we try them.

For instance, the number of people who become addicted to drugs is baffling, in spite of all the information and warnings about their dangers. They see what can happen to a person who is drug-addicted, and they can see the kinds of bad choices that an addicted person will often make to get the next fix. Some have even gone as far as prostituting or selling their own children to satisfy their cravings. It is also disheartening to see so many people choosing to smoke cigarettes or use other tobacco products in spite of what they presumably have heard about the long-term health consequences for smoking or using them. Others engage in extremely risky sexual behaviors that expose them to life-threatening diseases of which they must be aware, given the enormous amount of advertising and information about them. Ultimately, it is their choice!

We can become induced into destructive personal relationships and debilitating situations and can't quite figure how to get ourselves out of them. Many times we can have an intuitive sense from the beginning that they are bad for us, but the allure of their danger and forbidden nature can be exciting and intoxicating, thus blinding us from the reality of their potential, or near-certain, regrettable outcomes. These relationships and situations can have a profound negative impact on our sense of who we really are and what we should be doing with our time, talents and resources. Ignore a DO NOT ENTER sign on the Road of Life at your own peril!

One Way

ONE-WAY traffic, or uni-directional traffic, moves in one way or in a single direction. A one-way street is a street either facilitating only one-way traffic, or designed to direct vehicles to move in one direction. An advantage of one-way streets is that we do not have to watch for cars coming toward us from the opposite direction on this type of street. Many times on the Road of Life we will be asked to do something a particular way, even though it might be completely illogical to us and completely opposite to the way we see the world. In such instances, we may even dismiss the directive out-of-hand, calling it dumb, stupid or crazy. However, we have a choice of doing it that way or explaining why we think our way of doing it is better. We can choose to go in the opposite direction, but we must be aware of the friction and consequences we are likely to encounter when we do. We can question the directive, but we have to decide if opposing it outright is more advantageous than understanding the reason for the directive first and then figuring out how to change it if a change is really necessary. Once we understand the reason for the directive, we may come to the conclusion that the prescribed way, for numerous reasons, is superior to what we had in mind, or preferable to our way of thinking.

Road Closed

ROAD CLOSED signs are posted to let us know that movement beyond that point is prohibited. Quite often the specific reason for the prohibition is not specifically stated or conveyed.

On the Road of Life, there are many opportunities that others close to us for various and sundry reasons, and there are other roads that we should avoid or close to ourselves for our own good. We have to determine if an opportunity is actually closed or whether its closure is only a figment of our imagination, and we have to smart enough to know the difference between those decision points.

To be sure, others will deny us opportunities because of their biases, fears, prejudices and lack of personal development, but that should never be an excuse for us to sit and just look at the closed door. We should try to understand why the door is closed, who closed it, assess ourselves and our desire to open the door and explore all other avenues and options that are available to us. We may discover that the closed road was not the correct or most efficient portal for us anyway and that not entering it is the best decision for economic, political or strategic reasons. However, we should never allow our desire, knowledge, skills and abilities to be denied by others or limited by our perceptions that doors are closed when, in fact, they are open.

Just because a door is open doesn't mean that it is the door we should take or that it is an opportunity we should pursue in order to achieve our goals. We have to be wise enough to understand the difference.

Parking Prohibited

The "prohibition" symbol is used on traffic signs so that we can interpret traffic laws quickly while driving. The *no* symbol *(also prohibition sign, no sign, circle-backslash symbol, or universal no)* is a circle with a diagonal line through it (running from top left to bottom right), surrounding a pictogram used to indicate something is not permitted. The *no* symbol is usually colored red.

A NO PARKING sign is a prohibition against stopping our vehicle in that area and leaving it there. Implicit in a No Parking area is the high probability that our vehicle will be towed. Usually, there is no harm in pausing in the area for a few seconds and moving on.

On the Road of Life, there will be many signs prohibiting us from doing something, and it is important that we have the ability to recognize and avoid them. There are circumstances and situations that we should avoid at all cost. No matter how enticing some situations appear to be, they can be some of the most horrific pitfalls we can encounter. We have to learn when to slow down and look closely but move on without stopping. In some situations where we stop and park when we are not supposed to, tearing ourselves away from the clutches of unseen and unbeatable forces lurking there and moving forward again is nearly impossible.

Stop

STOP signs are used most often to control conflicting traffic movements at intersections, and they are installed mainly for safety and/or to assign the right-of-way for a certain direction because of the volume of traffic or the speed at which the traffic is approaching.

Sometimes on the Road of Life, we will be confronted with "cease and desist" orders, when means we have to stop whatever we are doing. We have to learn to just stop, stand still, and do nothing while there may be a bevy of activity occurring around us. Many self-help and motivational books tell us that we always should be moving forward, full-steam ahead, rolling over others if we have to. They tell us that we should block out all the distractions, any and everything that might prevent us from achieving our ultimate goals. If we're not moving constantly, they tell us, there must be something wrong with you. This is the height of arrogance. We can be very busy but still not make any progress. We can be moving constantly but still not be achieving our objectives or getting any closer to our goals.

The Bible tells us that, at times, we have to stand still and "see the salvation of the Lord." There are many battles in life that are not ours to fight. It says, "The Lord will fight for you, and you shall hold your peace." (Exodus 14: 13). We have to be discerning enough to recognize the stop signs in our life, smart enough to obey them and wise enough to know when to "Let go and let God."

Warnings

A traffic **warning sign** is a type of sign that indicates a hazard ahead on the road that may not be readily apparent to us. Warning signs can indicate any potential hazard, obstacle or condition requiring special attention. Warning signs call attention to conditions on, or adjacent to, a highway or street that are potentially hazardous to traffic operations. These signs are used particularly when the hazard is not obvious to us or we cannot see it.

Warning signs can indicate any potential hazard, obstacle or condition requiring special attention. General warning signs are used in instances in which the particular hazard, obstacle or condition is not covered by a standard sign. Traffic warning signs on our roads are important for alerting us to upcoming conditions or changes in traffic patterns that we need to be aware of. These signs help keep us safe by giving us fair warning of traffic and road conditions.

There are many warning signs on the Road of Life, alerting us of potentially hazardous conditions ahead, and signaling that we must do something out of the ordinary to maintain our course of travel. How and when we respond to warnings will determine whether our travel will be relatively easier or infinitely more difficult.

Be Prepared to Stop

A BE PREPARED TO STOP sign alerts us of potential hazards or the possibility that some unforeseen condition lies ahead. It means that we should slow down and be prepared to stop if necessary. Some reasons to be prepared to stop include:

- Crosswalks
- Railroad crossings
- Parked cars
- Pedestrians
- Children playing
- Construction sites
- Junctions where nobody has priority
- High concentration of emergency vehicles
- Snow storms and Blizzard conditions

We have to be prepared to stop on the Road of Life many times because we are approaching hazardous conditions, such as work overload, lack of quality time being spent with family and loved-ones, and the need for some mental health downtime. We often have to prepare ourselves to cut back on our relentless pursuit of our goals if we are unintentionally creating conditions that will preclude us from achieving those goals. We may have to re-assess what we are doing and why we are doing it. We may need to acquire some additional information that we didn't know we needed until we reached another milestone in our pursuit of our goal. We may need to get additional buy-in from key decision-makers, a spouse or a significant other who can have a significant impact on our ability to reach our goals. We may even have to consider reversing a decision, proceeding on a slightly different course or going in a totally different direction.

Some reasons to be prepared to stop on the Road of Life are:

- Lack of needed emotional support from loved ones
- Too many distractions to keep focused on goals and objectives
- Unfamiliar players in business dealings
- Insufficient information to make important decisions
- Need for additional technical understanding of an issue

We may have to prepare to stop until we have garnered support from allies or colleagues who can make the difference between success or failure in risk-prone ventures. We learn from these experiences that, if we don't at least prepare to stop, moving beyond those potential obstructions will make for difficulty going ahead.

Stop if you must, but never lose sight of where you are going.

Winding Road

The WINDING ROAD sign warns us that the road ahead has 3 or more closely-spaced curves or turns and bends in it, and that we may need to slow down to get through them safely. The sign signals that the road is twisting from a direct line or an even surface. A winding road is often full of surprises not only because of its circuitous, rambling and wandering nature, but also because of its blind spots and tortuous contours. Winding roads are usually found in hilly or mountainous areas where our view of what is coming is obstructed. A winding road represents the path of life, in that it does not lead by a straight line or course to a desired destination or outcome. We cannot predict what will come from a blind spot or area hidden from lack of clarity. Many blind spots and unexpected distractions that come into our path of travel can force us to make sudden and unsafe maneuvers.

Driving on winding roads can be a great deal of fun because of the exhilarating swings and sways of our vehicle as it travels along the road. On the other hand, it can be equally as dangerous because of the unexpected dangers that can pop up at the most inopportune time.

Many times we can be cruising merrily along the Road of Life and suddenly come upon signs warning us that there are twists and turns ahead and that we are likely to lose control if we don't slow down, re-assess and make the necessary adjustments to navigate the road ahead. We can be lulled into complacency and inattention because life is going so well for us, and we are riding high from our sense of well-being. The swings and sways can actually heighten our sense of success and invincibility, and cause us to have no qualms about throwing caution to the wind. However, if we are to have continuing success on the Road of Life, we cannot allow our easy rides to also become the source of our derailment or demise.

Curve or Curve Ahead

Any road sign that is yellow first indicates that it is a warning road sign. If it also has a black right curve on it, this means there is a sharp right curve ahead and we should slow down when approaching the curve.

A CRUVE or CURVE AHEAD sign does not always state that a reduction in the normal road speed is in order. Sharp turns, hairpin curves, broken back S-curves and other "non-standard" geometries can be found on roads. Curves and turns on rural roads can often be tricky for drivers to negotiate, as the safe speed may be considerably lower than the safe speed on the straightaway approaching the curve. As our vehicle approaches a curve, we hope that we will slow to an appropriate speed to safely negotiate the curve. However, this isn't always the case. The most frequently reported crashes and the most serious crashes on rural roads occur at curves and turns. These are usually a single vehicle run-off-the-road crash involving a driver entering the curve at excessive speed and losing control.

The attentive driver will know automatically that slowing down is the wise thing to do. Trying to slow down while in a curve is difficult to do, in addition to being dangerous. We can negotiate a curve much more successfully if we slow down *before* we get to it, not while we are in it. We can see the lay of the road and are better able to determine the speed at which we should proceed. The sign provides visual information about the nature of the curve we are approaching, letting us know whether it's a gradual curve, a sharp turn, a hairpin turn or some combination. Usually we are given fair warning that there are curves ahead, and we are allowed enough time to reduce our speed and to determine how we will approach them. If we ignore the sign, we won't anticipate the curves until we are already in them.

Many times on the Road of Life we have to slow down in order to negotiate successfully the challenges and opportunities that lie ahead. The uncertainties of challenges and opportunities should signal to us to slow down, but not stop, and to proceed with caution. By the time we arrive at the crucial point of travel, we'll have all that we need to negotiate the road ahead. If we choose to ignore the warning and maintain our normal way or speed of dealing with the issues before us, we decrease our chances of coming out of those situations in an optimal manner and feeling whole and having a sense of emotional well-being.

Dead End

While a DEAD END literally means that, at a certain point no additional forward movement can be made safely or without consequences. We can falsely believe that we are exempted from such warnings. Whether it is an inappropriate relationship or an unwise business arrangement we are about to enter into, the warning sign is often tugging at our conscience, giving us an uneasy feeling and telling us that the arrangement will lead eventually to circumstances that are unhealthy for us—emotionally, financially, professionally or spiritually. The sign tells us to change our course of direction, either reverse our forward movement, or go left or go right. If we choose to continue on the dead-end path, the eventual outcome is unlikely to be pleasant.

Many of us spend too many precious years of our lives and too much of our valuable time going down dead-end roads, chasing dreams and opportunities that seem too good to be true. When we come to the realization that the road is a dead-end, sometimes it is hard for us to accept it as a fool's errand because of all the emotional investment we have in the journey. We haven't developed the mental maturity or the interpersonal relationship skills required to stand off in the distance, do a thoughtful analysis, and see that the road ahead is leading nowhere before we get on it. We will make a lot of assumption but ask no questions.

Rather than take a real hard look at ourselves and our behaviors when we find that we're headed toward a dead-end, we are likely to blame others for our failure to recognize and understand that where we are going is leading somewhere we don't want to go. Unfortunately, we can find ourselves in situations where there is no easy or graceful way out once we get there. Unlike a One-Way street, which allows us to at least go one way, a DEAD END leaves us with few options. There's usually no direct way out, and often there is nowhere to turn around. Therefore, avoiding those dead-ends on the Road of Life is

Merging

MERGING signs are posted for a variety of reasons. Merging, literally, means joining. More traffic may be going to join the roadway and drive along the same lane. Some other reasons for merging are ONE LANE BRIDGE, ROAD NARROWS, LAND ENDS MERGE RIGHT/LEFT, LANE REDUCTION AND DIVIDED HIGHWAY ENDS. When we see a merging car ahead, we should signal and move over to the other lane if we can safely change lanes.

Sometimes the driver in the merging car has to yield, slow down and wait for a safe gap in highway traffic.

- Lane Reduction Transition
- Lane Ends Merge Right/Left
- Road Narrows
- Narrow Bridge
- One Lane Bridge
- Divided Highway Begins
- Divided Highway Ends
- Two Way Traffic

These signs warn us that the lane in which we are driving

will be merging into another, requiring extra caution and the possibility of a speed reduction or increase. Merge signs call for extra courtesy to those who will be merging into our lane and if we are merging into theirs.

Teaming up with or joining forces with others allows us to capitalize on the force multiplier effect of collaboration, even with people with whom we have very little, if anything, in common. Combining, merging or pooling our resources with others teach us how to share expertise, information and knowledge. It is through such merging or collaborating that we learn from others how to develop or enhance or skills and abilities and they can learn from us. This can lay the foundation for everlasting friendships, and it can create opportunities for to learn how to give without expecting anything in return.

Detour Ahead

The DETOUR AHEAD sign tells us that our usual route is closed and that we will have to take a different one, a digression that will probably take us longer to reach our destination than traveling on our intended course. The DETOUR AHEAD sign is common on many roads. In fact, it is unusual to complete a journey of any significance without having to take a few detours here and there. DETOUR AHEAD means that a diversion has been put in place farther up the road, and therefore serves as a warning that we will be diverted from the usual route as a result. It also means that the road is closed ahead of us and traffic is being routed onto other roads to bypass the area that is closed. This type of detour is official because it has been specifically chosen for traffic to follow. In theory, there will be signs that say "Detour," with an arrow pointing the way along the route. In practice, it's very easy for us to miss a sign and get lost.

On the Road of Life, we may have to make many detours if we expect to reach our final destination successfully. Detours can be energizing and healthy. They often allow us to avoid circumstances and situations we otherwise would have to face if we stayed on our normal course. They can aid us in finding a new mental and physical resolve for getting back on the main Road of Life. While we often complain about detours, they can be exactly what we need to give us a different, broader and more informed perspective. The hum-drum of the main Road of Life can blind us to other opportunities and possibilities. Detours can force us to be more self-reflective. In fact, the detours may be the exact thing God wants us to do because we're on the wrong road, but we just don't know it yet, or we just haven't quite figured it out. God is putting us where we *need* to be, but not necessarily where we *want* to be. It also may be that we're being directed away from or around some impending disaster or cataclysmic situation.

Detours can be the very thing we need to intervene in our lives because they can speed maturity, develop our character and make us a better, stronger and more understanding person. Sometimes in life, we are not emotionally ready for the things God has for us or the things that are about to happen for us or to us. Sometimes we have to spend time in a few deserts, dark places and valleys before we arrive at our destination. We have to be seasoned, get our egos in check, and learn compassion and humility before we come back to the main route that's leading us to our desired destination. Many times, it is only then that we can appreciate and endure the important things that we are about to experience. It is on those detours, or long ways around, that we often have to travel for God to show us His incredible power, as He did repeatedly with many Old Testament giants like the Israelites, Moses, David, and Elijah.

Detours can force us to face and overcome our greatest challenges and deepest fears. On the other hand, a detour can put us on an alternate route we would rather avoid. If we are able to anticipate a detour in sufficient time, we can stop, reverse our course and take the alternate route of our choosing.

Life can be moving along smoothly and, suddenly, we come to a DETOUR AHEAD sign. Something happens that we weren't expecting; something doesn't work out the way we had planned or we may just lose our focus and momentum. Detours can come in many forms, such as the loss of a house to foreclosure, the end of a long-time love relationship, the closure of a business where we worked for many years.

This just means that we may have to take another path to reach the same goal that we were aiming at in the first place. It doesn't mean that we have failed; it just means that we might have to take a bit more time or it may be a bit more uncomfortable than originally thought. We have to be careful not to turn our detours into dead ends.

Sometimes we may even find that some detours end up taking us a better way than our original route. There are many and varied ways to achieve and reach what we desire. Some detours may appear as a sign to actually get us back on the right path as we may have been way off track. As with any detour that we may find when they are placed on the road, we make sure we watch out for the signs to show us the right way to go, otherwise we may end up getting lost and in a place that we didn't want to go to in the first place.

Sometimes we may be traveling down the Road of Life and heading towards our goals and, all of a sudden, we come across a detour. While we all may think that we have worked things out to the finest detail, life just doesn't work that way. If success were easy, then everyone would be successful.

That is why we need to be prepared for those detours. Many of us seem to assume that there is just one way, our way, to success. Well, the fact is that there are probably many ways to achieve what we want. This means that we must make sure we are open to change and that making a dreaded change, in fact, is probably the best way to achieve what we want.

To be sure, coming across a detour really isn't a fun experience because it can have the tendency to make us feel as though we are taking two steps forward and one step backwards, but as long as we press on, we *are* making incremental progress. We can take detours voluntarily for a variety of reasons when no DETOUR AHEAD signs are anywhere in sight.

Hill

A traffic sign with only the word HILL on it can be confusing if we don't know whether we're heading toward a peak or toward a valley. We don't know if the road ahead is ascending or going up, or descending or going down, or if we don't have an intuitive sense of the direction of our travel or know the lay of the land. In either instance, we will have to adjust our travel in anticipation of successfully negotiating the terrain immediately ahead, whether it is up or down.

If the sign shows that the road is ascending or going up, we know that we will probably have to accelerate if we want to maintain your current speed and to reach the summit of the hill without a lot of strain. If the sign shows that the road is descending or going down, it is natural to decelerate, to "take your foot off the gas," or to coast.

The hills on the Road of Life pose similar conditions for us. If we are fortunate, we will be able to discern if the travel ahead is going up or going down. The hills causing the greatest challenge, of course, are those requiring the most use of our personal investments—emotional, financial, and physical, etc.—to ascend. Those hills require us to pay close attention and to exert focused effort if we are to succeed. However, we can have our greatest catastrophes while all is going well for us. While the journey is markedly easier, we are prone to take our "eye of the ball," lose focus and go with the flow. Life is easy; worries are few; because things are going our way. Therefore, slowing down is not among our instinctive reactions to such a confluence of positive factors. It is during such times that we miss important clues, cues and signals we need to keep us on track and on target. It is important to savor our time on "easy street," but we must not allow the ride to derail the journey.

Use Low Gear

The USE LOW GEAR sign is usually a warning for truck drivers who are going down hill to use a lower gear because it will hold the vehicle back. This will allow the vehicle to descend a hill at a slower and safer speed. If a truck or another vehicle travels too fast downhill, the driver could easily lose control of it. It is assumed that the average individual would know to slow down automatically when going down a steep hill, but some individuals have to be warned.

Many times in life, when things are going extremely well, we have to put ourselves in a lower gear to calm our euphoria and exuberance without killing our enthusiasm. The lower gear will allow us the opportunity to slow down, to think things through and not to become distracted by our achievements and successes.

Sometimes on the Road of Life, it is almost certain that we will have to use a lower gear to assist us in climbing a hill. While the lower gear gives us more power to move methodically upward, it can also assists us is slowing down or reducing our speed as we move downward.

When we use a lower gear, or dig a little deeper into our personal reserves and reservoirs as we travel on the Road of

Life, it gives us the additional torque or energy we need to tackle temporary setbacks and challenging situations head-on and to find the confidence to know that challenges may be difficult but not impossible to overcome. The lower gear can allow us to tap into our reservoirs of belief, determination and self-reliance, and to develop the emotional strength and mental toughness to travel with greater ease and self-assurance.

Rough Road

A ROUGH ROAD sign warns drivers that the road ahead is deficient or unsuitable for the normal speed of travel and, importantly, that bumps, dips, sink holes, uneven areas or washboard surfaces in the road could damage our speeding vehicle. ROUGH ROAD signs are used often in advance of road construction areas, and they are great for roads that are crossed by overflow streams or that lack pavement. We are warned about rough road surfaces because they can cause us a lot of motion discomfort, and they could cause us to lose control of the vehicle.

The Road of Life is filled with many rough areas or patches, but we are able to travel over them with grace, dignity and resolve if we stay the course. There may be times that we really feel like throwing up our hands in frustration and resignation, believing that no matter what we do is of little or no use. There may be times that we are unable to take care of all our personal and financial obligations. Our spouse or significant other may not understand us or is inattentive to our emotional needs. Co-workers and acquaintances may not treat us with the same level of professionalism and respect as they do others.

Regardless of the rough terrains we encounter on the Road of Life, we can usually get over them successfully if we realize that many difficulties are only temporary. We also have to realize that others will often create difficulty situations for us, not because of who we are but because of who they are. Their personal issues can become the center-piece of their existence. However, we must not internalize their personal issues and make them ours. If we do, we unconsciously are likely to finds ways to maneuver ourselves onto many rough roads along the journey and to convince ourselves that we like and probably deserve it.

Loose Gravel

A LOOSE GRAVEL signs mean that the road surface is covered with a loose mixture of pebbles and rock fragments coarser than sand, and the gravel is often mixed with clay. Loose gravel can cause our vehicle to lose control and skid, kicking up road surface materials that can land on another vehicle. The gravel also can be thrown onto our windshield by another car. A LOOSE GRAVEL SIGN is a signal for us to reduce our speed and to proceed carefully. A reduction in speed allows the vehicle to maintain a secure footing on the road surface.

We are likely to encounter many rough patches on the Road of Life that have loose gravel, causing us to lose our emotional anchor and psychological footing and to lose our desired bearing if we are not careful. We can become devastated by the betrayal of people we thought were our friends. We can learn about the unfaithfulness of a spouse or significant other, or the intentional and willful use of innuendo and misleading information meant to hurt us. These are acts that can shake our core beliefs about many things in life we've considered sacrosanct. They can leave us with bitter tastes and urges to exact revenge. But, we have to learn that encountering loose gravel on the Road of Life is no reason for us to abandon our ethical standard and moral principles. We learn from the warnings and telltale signs that it's time for us to slow down, pay attention and recalibrate our thinking and our actions.

No Outlet

A NO OUTLET signs means that the road of travel leads to a dead-end street or enclosed area. There is no other street leading out, other than the way we came in. The road ends, and there are no streets branching off of it or connecting to it. It means that we cannot drive continuously through this particular area or neighborhood. The one we're on is the only entrance/exit to the area We will eventually have to come back where we came in to get back where we started. If we travel down a dead end street at some point we will have to make a 'U' turn and come back to the intersection with the sign. A dead-end corridor is much like a dead end street, in that it intersects a main corridor, restricts movement, and has no other outlet to other corridors or exits.

On the Road of Life, we are likely to come upon many situations we can easily enter into, but find nearly impossible to get ourselves out of. While the NO EXIT or NO OUTLET signs give us adequate warning, we often have difficulties seeing how to retreat from the danger of them because of our inattention, or our mistaken belief that the signs are not meant for us. We may even believe that if we enter the path we were warned about, we are able to get out because we are smarter and wiser than others, and will never suffer the same fate of those who are less savvy and more timid than we.

No Passing Zone

A NO PASSING ZONE sign, which is always on the opposite side of the road, signals a warning that we are approaching an area where there is potential danger. While we cannot yet see or imagine the danger, it's still there. We are to maintain our current position and proceed with caution. No passing is allowed when approaching within 100 feet of any underpass or tunnel, railroad grade crossing, intersection within a city, or intersection outside of a city if the presence of the intersection is marked by warning signs. It means that we cannot pass any vehicles in that zone. It can also signify that the passing zone has ended.

On the Road of Life, there are times when a No Passing Zones sign makes us feel more compelled to charge ahead and pass anything and anybody who is traveling at a pace that is too slow for our liking. We may not be able to "see" anything ahead that can interrupt our travel, but we may not realize that what lies ahead doesn't always have to be seen in order to interrupt our journey or quench our desire to move ahead. For instance, we can fight for a promotion *we* believe we've earned and deserve, but not realize our knowledge, skills and abilities are not sufficient for us to be successful in the assignment. Others may suspect or know that, but they have not found the courage to share that assessment with us because they know we are not likely to receive such information in the spirit it was given. Predictably, we can be a miserable failure in the assignment, or we literally can burn ourselves out, or work ourselves into a frazzle, trying to prove to ourselves and others that we got the promotion on our merit. We must learn that there is no harm in being patient and that passing in a NO PASSING zone can be detrimental and unforgiving.

Crosswinds

A CROSSWINDS sign or flying sock symbol, as indicated by a windsock on red triangle or yellow diamond signs, indicates locations where a strong side wind may cause the trajectory of a moving vehicle to change drastically, perhaps even "flying" across lanes, causing an accident. Strong cross winds can move cars, motorcycle and trucks out of their lanes of travel, and they can blow across the course or path of a ship, aircraft, etc., sometimes with considerable force, from an area of high pressure to an area of low pressure.

While traveling on the Road of Life, we will encounter many crosswinds that appear to come unexpectedly from nowhere, dropping drama and trauma on anybody and anything in sight. They can be conflicts others caused because of their inability or lack of desire to work with us for childish or frivolous reasons. Crosswinds can result from misunderstandings in past relationship that were never completely resolved, and can resurface and grow in intensity every time there is any kind of interpersonal interaction with the individual. There can be crosswinds from inter-group rivalries or intra-group conflicts at our place of employment, and they can inflict enormous emotional pain and blow individuals and organizations off-track when they are allowed to persist. There can be crosswinds between couples who have different and competing goals and objectives or have difficulty understanding each other's motives. Any turbulence caused by crosswinds is not likely to subside until some action is taken or something is said to balance out or normalize the pressure that is causing the crosswinds.

Crosswinds that keep pushing us off track and requiring us to expend energy to right ourselves on the Road of Life must be avoided. To the extent that we can anticipate those crosswinds and take the appropriate actions to blunt or dissipate them before they cross our paths, the more able we are to travel uninterrupted and with confidence.

Severe Strom Area

SEVERE STORM AREA signs are posted to warn us of the occurrence or imminent threats of violent tornadoes and damaging thunderstorms. The occurrence, location and timing may still be uncertain, but these weather conditions can produce sizable hail, destructive winds, frequent and intense cloud-to-ground lightning, and torrential rains causing significant visibility restrictions, especially near major highways during high traffic times or "ponding" of water on roadways. Some SEVERE STORM AREA signs are posted to warn us of fog, dust storms and snowstorms because the weather conditions can cause visibility restrictions. Dam failures often result from severe storms, and ice dams often result from snowstorms, interrupting the normal flow of water.

While traveling the Road of Life, we are fortunate if we never experience or never enter into any severe storm areas. Some stormy areas of life can include the loss of a loved one, a child, or a parent; a sudden physical ailment or the diagnosis of a debilitating disease; the loss of a job or source of income; a new boss who is difficult to work with; a hostile working environment and contentious working relationships that resulted from new co-workers joining our organization. We can be bombarded with an onslaught of misfortunes resulting from circumstances over which we have no control. These storms can either derail us or make us stronger.

We know that dealing with some people will cause a storm no matter how hard we try to have harmonious relationships with them. They are people we should avoid if possible, or if we have an alternate course of action.

Slides

A SLIDES sign indicates that we are in an area where rock, earth, or debris flows on slopes due to gravity. They can occur on any terrain given the right conditions of soil, moisture, and the angle of the slope. Integral to the natural process of the earth's surface geology, landslides serve to redistribute soil and sediments in a process that can be in abrupt collapses or in slow gradual slides. Such is the nature of the earth's surface dynamics. Also known as mud flows, debris flows, earth failures, slope failures, etc., they can be triggered by rains, floods, earthquakes, and other natural causes as well as human-made causes, such as grading, terrain cutting and filling, excessive development, etc. Because the factors affecting landslides can be geophysical or human-made, they can occur in developed areas, undeveloped areas, or any area where the terrain was altered for roads, houses, utilities, buildings, and even for lawns in one's backyard.

Very much like the typical road or highway, the Road of Life can be filled with many unanticipated and unforeseen challenges and life-changing events. That's just the way life is because of the dynamic nature of human behavior and the organic nature of uncontrollable circumstances. All types of flows can end up across our paths, and they have nothing to do with us and our specific actions. It is up to us to deal with each one with the expectation that it is not the end of life's journey. Some situations that can trigger storms in our lives are:

- Loss of a parent
- A separation or divorce
- Heartbreak
- An unjustified termination of employment
- A terminal illness

Slides usually block our path completely or partially, oftentimes leaving us with no way to move forward from that juncture until something or someone steps in and clears our path. We can experience emotional crosswinds such as doubts about our professional competence, our insecurities with our personal abilities and attributes or lack of confidence in our communication skills.

In spite of the crosswinds that may blow into our path of travel, we can endure the disturbances by hanging onto our core beliefs and values, and we must have faith that such troubles will not last forever.

5 Markers, Guides and Information

When we're planning a trip, we want to know the best route to take. We have to decide if we want to travel the Interstate Highway, US. Highway/Secondary or County Highway/ Service Road System, or a combination of all three. And if we want to go safely, and save time and travel costs at the same time, we should plan our trip carefully, using a sophisticated GPS (global positioning system) or a good road map. Each route shown on the map is marked by a number. The route number on the map corresponds with the numbers posted on the highway. Therefore, by choosing from the map the route we want to take, we can reach our chosen destination simply by following the numbers posted on the highway. There are several different highway systems. The routes in each system are posted with a particular type of marker.

Guide signs show route designations, distances, services, points of interest, and other geographical, recreational, or cultural information. Destination guide signs typically have white lettering on a green background. Service and recreational signs have blue and brown backgrounds, respectively. Other guide signs such as route designations may use a variety of colors depending on the type of road and state or local practice.

To the extent that we recognize and can understand the markers, guides and information posted along the Road of Life, the better positioned we are to travel with surprising ease. We have to decide where we want to go and plan our journey in a manner that will allow us to reach our destination by way of our desired route. In spite of the planning we do, there are sure to be many circumstances and situations that will interrupt our journey and impede our progress—that's just how life is. However, if we don't have some kind of plan or trip map, imagine just how much more difficult life could be.

Mileposts

Green and white mileposts are posted at one-mile intervals along the Interstate routes. They tell us the progress we are making. Since they are placed at one-mile intervals along the route, they are also useful in reporting locations of accidents, disabled vehicles and other emergencies. A **milestone** is one of a series of numbered markers placed along a road or boundary at one-mile intervals or, occasionally, parts of a mile. They are typically located at the side of the road or in a median and are alternatively known as **mile markers**, **mileposts** (sometimes abbreviated **MPs**). **Mileage** is the distance along the road from a fixed starting point.

Milestones are constructed to provide reference points along the road. They can be used to reassure us that we are following the proper path, and to indicate either the distance we have traveled or the remaining distance we have to travel before reaching our destination. These references are also used by emergency services and road maintenance personnel to direct them to specific points where they are needed. This term is sometimes used to denote a location on a road even if no physical sign is present. This is useful for accident reporting and other record keeping.

On the Road of Life, goals and timelines are similar to milestones, mile markers and mile posts. They help to keep us focused and on schedule, making it easier for us to expend the effort required to achieve those goals. Research has shown repeatedly that people who have clearly defined goals, and who work diligently toward them, usually accomplish much more in life than those individuals who have no goals at all.

If we have clearly defined goals we are trying to achieve along the Road of Life, and know exactly where we are relative to attaining them, we can often be surprised by the assistance others are willing to give us if we ask. But, if we don't have any goals, we won't know what we need.

By - Pass

A BYPASS is a road or highway that avoids or "bypasses" a built-up area, town, or village, to let through traffic flow without interference from local traffic, to reduce congestion in the built-up area, and to improve road safety. A "Business" sign means the route leads through the town's business area. The BYPASS is normally a faster route.

On the Road of Life, we have to make decisions about whether to travel a by-pass to avoid congested and built-up areas or to remain on a major road or highway. Travel in a congested area requires us to pay close attention, interact and be involved with others, as well as move at a slower pace. If we avoid the Interstate Highway System and always travel on the secondary road, it undoubtedly will take us longer to reach our destination, but we are more likely to have opportunities to experience the local color, encounter people who make indelible impressions on us, and learn to appreciate the inter-connectedness of all humanity.

We may be afraid to travel the Interstate Highway System because we are afraid of the speed at which everybody is probably travelling, and are more adept at travelling on secondary roads or are always looking for a "Business" route to take. As savvy travelers on the Road of Life, we have to develop the skills and abilities to move comfortably along both routes and to exercise the judgment to know which route to take and when.

Scenic Overlook Ahead

Along most Interstate Highways and Secondary roads, there are numerous conveniences and friendly diversions to help make our journey more enjoyable. There are fantastic scenic overviews of valleys, pleasant rest and recreational areas, luscious picnic areas; convenient roadside parks, natural trails and many more. These and diversions allow us opportunities for rejuvenation and relaxation. Many of the scenic views display near-breathless experiences of beauty, diversity and natural wonders, as can be seen in the following locations:

- Oregon Coast Highway from Astoria on Route 101
- Monument Valley in Arizona
- Blue Ridge Parkway and Skyline Drive in North Carolina and Virginia
- Pacific Coast Highway on Route 1 in California
- Beartooth Highway in Montana and Wyoming
- Shiprock in New Mexico
- Devils Tower in Wyoming
- Natural Bridge, Virginia
- Stone Mountain, Georgia
- The Wave on the border of Arizona and Utah

While travelling on the Road of Life, we should exit occasionally to take advantages of the many opportunities to relax and rejuvenate ourselves. The activities, amenities and diversions we find and experience allow us to take a breather from the stresses and strains of daily living, and they help us to gain a different perspective on the efficacy and progress of our journey. We can see and experience the diversity of life and the natural wonders God has provided for us to enjoy. More importantly, we can witness the unbelievable display of His awesome power, unlimited resources and expansive province. The views and vistas hold the capacity to totally transform us.

Restraining ourselves from overly indulging in all of life's awesome beauty and friendly diversions can be difficult if we are undisciplined. There are enticing scenic views and frivolous opportunities at numerous exits on the Road of Life. If we are not careful, we will spend our most productive years taking in the views and engaging in meaningless frivolities when we should be traveling with a determined and focused destination in mind. We don't want the beautiful views and enjoyable distractions to consume so much of our time and energies that we don't realize until late that our life's journey is nearing an end. We need to be wise in how we balance the use of our time with the quality of our choices.

Afterword

We all are on the Road of Life, and we have not always known where that road was leading us and what conditions we were likely to encounter. In its own way, each person's Road is unique to that individual, but there are many experiences that we all have in common and circumstances that parallel each other, the good as well as the bad. In spite of the differences and similarities, most of us learn from our varied pleasant and painful experiences, especially if we adhere to the clues telling us what lies ahead and if we are attuned to the feedback that helps us to assess those situations in our past—the road we have traveled. When we dismiss the clues and feedback as inaccessible tools beyond our immediate grasp and unrealistic ideals outside the realm of our true selves, the Road of Life is unlikely and unwilling to allow us to have a charmed, easy and relatively stress-free journey.

While our Road of Life may not end exactly on our terms, it will end, nevertheless. Our conditions and circumstances at that point of our journey will be determined by the quality of our choices along the way, how we responded to the many factors beyond our control, and how we managed the many factors that were within our sphere of personal influence.

If we learn to navigate and negotiate our way successfully along the Road of Life, the journey will take us very close to where we want to be. No matter where we are on the journey, the Traffic Signs on the Road of Life are always present, instructing, warning, marking and guiding us along the way. It is our choice to learn and to obey them in order to remove the barriers to our personal growth and success, or ignore them and suffer the consequences. Barriers to growth and success are like dams. Once removed, the river of growth flows unfettered by the dam that held it back, and the likelihood of success increases. Those barriers are as diverse as people, but we usually know what they are in our lives.

Therefore, the question is not about not knowing the signs; it is in determining what we are going to do about them—precisely because we don't want to crash or stall out in our growth and development while we're on the Road of Life.

About the Authors

Cynthia Waters-Brower is an educator, technology facilitator and a minister. She is the founder and publisher of PwP Publishing, which specializes in preparing manuscripts for publication; designing and developing websites, and publishing memorial program materials. Mrs. Brower is a former corporate manager in the areas of accounting, purchasing and procurement. She has worked an Instructional Facilitator and currently is an Instructional Designer for the North Carolina Department of Instruction. She is a graduate of University of North Carolina-Greensboro with a Bachelor's Degree in Business Administration, Oral Roberts University with a Master's Degree in Practical Theology, and the University of North Dakota with a Master's Degree in Instructional Design and Technology.

Wilbur Brower, Ph.D., is an educational and management consultant and trainer, and founder and president of W. Brower & Associates. He is also the founder and president of the Institute for Youth Development and Educational Resources (IYDER), Inc., a non-profit that works with students at-risk of academic and personal failure. Dr. Brower served in the U. S. Air Force, and he is a former corporate executive with a Fortune 100 company.

He is the author of *A Little Book of Big Principles—Values and Virtues for a More Successful Life* (1998); *Me Teacher, Me...Please! Observations about Parents, Students and*

Teachers, and the Teacher-Learning Process (2002); and *English Grammar and Writing Made Easy* (2008). He is the co-author of *Personal Care Journal—The Adult Years* (2002).

www.ingramcontent.com/pod-product-compliance
Lightning Source LLC
LaVergne TN
LVHW010941110826
845149LV00013B/2698

* 9 7 8 0 9 8 8 4 4 9 0 0 8 *